A STUDY GUIDE BASED ON THE BOOK

The Perfect LOVE

RUTH MYERS

WATERBROOK
PRESS

COLORADO SPRINGS

A Study Guide
to THE PERFECT LOVE by Ruth Myers
PUBLISHED BY WATERBROOK PRESS
5446 North Academy Boulevard, Suite 200
Colorado Springs, Colorado 80918
A division of Bantam Doubleday Dell Publishing Group, Inc.

Quotations from *The Perfect Love:* © 1998 by Ruth Myers

ISBN 1-57856-083-7

Printed in the United States of America
1998 — First Edition

10 9 8 7 6 5 4 3 2 1

This Is Real Love

*A companion Bible study to Chapters 1 and 2
in THE PERFECT LOVE*

I'm trusting that… you have this same longing deep
within, even as I do: We *must* have love. We must have
God's love. We must have *God*, the only source of perfect,
unfailing love. I believe God has sovereignly brought you
and me together at this time and through these pages,
wanting to bless us in the adventure of letting Him fulfill
our heart cry.

—Ruth Myers in *THE PERFECT LOVE*

---

1. How would you express in your own words your
   personal desire for a deeper knowledge of God and
   His love?

On this question and throughout this study guide, you may
want to express all your answers in words addressed directly to
God. You can think of your answers as your part of an ongoing
personal conversation with God your loving Father.

In one way or another, we so often assume that God is like us. We fashion Him after our own image or after the image of other imperfect people we know....

The most important part of living realistically is to hold a true view of God. God is ultimate reality. He's the greatest factor in all that's real. When we let the truth about Him nourish us and remold our minds, this revolutionizes our lives.

—Ruth Myers in *THE PERFECT LOVE*

2. Take a close and personal look at 1 John 4:16. Think carefully about these words from God's heart. Then summarize what this passage tells us about how we can respond to God's love, and why.

Throughout this study guide, you may find it particularly rewarding to look up passages in more than one Scripture version. As a start, use one basic translation, such as *The New International Version*, *The New American Standard Bible*, or *The New King James Version*, and supplement it with one or two other translations or paraphrases, such as *The New Living Translation*, *The New Century Version*, *The Good News Bible*, or J. B. Phillips's *New Testament in Modern English*. Later you may want to explore some of the following: *The Amplified Bible*, *The Berkeley Version in Modern English*, *The New English Bible*, and *The Revised Standard Version*, as well as versions by Ronald Knox, Frank C. Laubach, James Moffatt, Eugene H. Peterson, R. F. Weymouth, Charles B. Williams, and Kenneth S. Wuest.

3. Reflect deeply on Paul's prayer for the Ephesian Christians in Ephesians 3:17-19. How would you reword this now as your own personal prayer?

4. Do the same with the prayer words of Moses in Psalm 90:14, expressing it as your personal prayer.

God has given us in His Word a beautiful picture of what His steadfast love is like. He wants to speak His love to our hearts, individually, tenderly. He wants you to take time to hear His words of love, and to let them dawn on you undimmed, that you may very soon be satisfied... and be glad all your days.

—Ruth Myers in THE PERFECT LOVE

---

5. Outline here your plan for completing all of this study guide on *The Perfect Love* (schedule set-aside times for your study and reflection each week), then commit your plan to the Lord in a written prayer.

> If we want real love, ideal love, perfect love, God's heart is where to find it. It's the only love big enough to meet the God-sized needs of your life and mine.
>
> —Ruth Myers in *THE PERFECT LOVE*

6. Meditate on what these Scripture passages tell us about the greatness of God's love, and record your thoughts.

   (In various English versions of the Old Testament, the rich Hebrew word *hesed* is translated in several different ways—including "love," "lovingkindness," "steadfast love," "unfailing love," "mercy," "goodness," "kindness," and so on. This rich term is the strongest and most common Old Testament word for God's love. It is found in each of the verses below as well as in several Scriptures used throughout this study guide, so you may want to remember the various ways it is translated.)

   a. Psalm 33:5

   b. Psalm 36:5

   c. Psalm 86:15

   d. Psalm 100:5

> God offers us a perfect and permanent love, a love
> relationship that can meet our deepest needs at every
> point of life and forever. And He wants us to respond to
> His love. In His heart He is intensely involved with us.
>
> I wonder if we are intensely involved with Him?
>
> —Ruth Myers in *THE PERFECT LOVE*

7. Carefully write out **Psalm 90:14** in the space below, then begin committing this passage to memory.

In time alone with God, review what you have written down and learned in this lesson.

Perhaps you sense something here that God wants you to especially understand and trust Him for at this time. If so, go back and mark it in the lesson, then bring it again before the Lord in prayer and grateful praise.

Record here any further thoughts or prayer requests that come to your mind and heart.

His Eternal Longings Coming True

*A companion Bible study to Chapter 3
in The Perfect Love*

God is always yearning for us and always has been.

—Ruth Myers in THE PERFECT LOVE

---

1. How do the following passages indicate that God has always been yearning for relationship with His people, and always will be?

   a. Matthew 25:34

   b. Ephesians 1:4

   c. Ephesians 1:11-12

   d. Ephesians 2:4-7

e. Revelation 21:1-4

There was a time when I was troubled by the command
that Jesus says is first and greatest — that we should love
the Lord our God with all our heart and soul and mind
and strength. It made me feel uncomfortable and guilty. I
wanted to love God this much, and I liked to think I
sometimes did. Yet I knew I didn't all the time, and
perhaps I never achieved it. I loved Him more than I
loved anyone else, but love Him with *all* my heart and
soul and mind and strength? No, I was so often distracted
or distrustful or drifting.

Some years ago I realized this is the most flattering and
complimentary verse in the Bible. I am so important to
God that He wants *me* to love Him totally.... Only if
someone means a great deal to us, only if we really love
that person, do we ask that.

—Ruth Myers in *THE PERFECT LOVE*

---

2. Take a personal look at Mark 12:30, and record here
   your grateful response to each portion of this
   "flattering and complimentary" command.

His love is not simply for mankind as a mass — not some sentimental, vague, diffused feeling.... No, God really likes individual people. His love is intensely personal.

—Ruth Myers in *THE PERFECT LOVE*

3. Notice in Galatians 2:20 how Paul indicated the intensely personal nature of God's love for him. Express the truth of this verse in your own words, as it applies to you.

Perhaps you easily remember that God has compassion for you and a willingness to help you. Or you may think of God as taking care of our needs in a somewhat condescending way — after all, we're His creatures, so He does His duty toward us. But maybe you've overlooked how intense His feelings really are — how He desires you, how much He finds delight whenever you cultivate your love relationship with Him as one who belongs to Him.

—Ruth Myers in *THE PERFECT LOVE*

4. How do the following passages show the way in which God enjoys His love relationship with His people?

a. Psalm 149:4

b. Isaiah 62:4-5

c. Zephaniah 3:17

I'm sure you're as astonished as I am that God can find such enjoyment from intimacy with us....

This amazing love, so undeserved, is indeed hard to grasp with our minds: God is so intimately and personally involved with me that He longs for my fellowship. But as someone has said, it is "darkness to my intellect but sunshine to my heart." You and I can actually bring God pleasure!...What better motivation can there be for spending time with Him day by day?

—Ruth Myers in *THE PERFECT LOVE*

---

5. Read the following verses in Song of Solomon (Song of Songs), and see and hear in these words a portrayal of the Lord's personal longing for you, His beloved one. Allow Him to express these words to you. Then record here your response to Him.

   a. 1:15

   b. 2:14

   c. 4:7

d. 4:10

We are God's treasure! This is one of the most exciting truths in the Bible.... *We* are *His* inheritance, *His* treasure — isn't this incredible?

—Ruth Myers in THE PERFECT LOVE

---

6. How do these passages portray God's people as His treasure and inheritance?

   a. Isaiah 62:3

   b. Malachi 3:16-17

   c. Ephesians 1:18

The Lord takes special pleasure in us as we respond to Him with love, worship, faith, and obedience. As we let Him be our chief treasure we bring Him those unique joys that no one else can bring. And we bring Him unique griefs as we ignore Him and speed through our days, giving Him little thought. Day by day, moment by moment, you and I determine whether He loves us with a glad love or a grieved love.

—Ruth Myers in THE PERFECT LOVE

---

7. For helpful review, write out **Psalm 90:14** from memory in the space below.

In time alone with God, review what you have written down and learned in this lesson.

Perhaps you sense something here that God wants you to especially understand and trust Him for at this time. If so, mark it in the lesson, then bring it again before the Lord in prayer and grateful praise.

Record here any further thoughts or prayer requests that come to your mind and heart.

Drawing Us Near

*A companion Bible study to Chapter 4
in The Perfect Love*

Because you are a special treasure to God, He is working
to draw you into a deeper love for Him — away from any
idols in your life, away from rival interests, away from
giving first place to His good gifts instead of to Him.

—Ruth Myers in *THE PERFECT LOVE*

---

1. In Jeremiah 31:3, what does God say His love for His
people has prompted Him to do?

I believe He grants all of us certain love-gifts that help us
come closer to Him and know Him better. Five of these
stand out to me as foundational to our love relationship
with Him: His Word, His indwelling Spirit, the body of
Christ, the circumstances of our daily lives, and the path
of obedience.

—Ruth Myers in *THE PERFECT LOVE*

Use the following questions to help you think about (and be
grateful for) the way in which God has directed the first four

of these love-gifts personally to you. (We'll explore the fifth love-gift, the path of obedience, in a later lesson.)

2. Ruth Myers writes, "The first love-gift is His Word, where we find our most beautiful and comprehensive portrait of Him." Express your gratitude here for what the Bible has meant to you as a personal gift of love from God your Father.

3. Now express your thanksgiving for the second love-gift—the indwelling presence of God's Holy Spirit. (Ruth Myers reminds us, "As we feed on God's Word, the Spirit empowers us to see and understand the Lord and His love.")

4. Record here your personal expression of gratefulness for His third love-gift to you—other believers in Christ.

5. Now let God know your appreciation for His fourth love-gift—the circumstances of your daily life. As Ruth Myers reminds us, "God so acutely wants to enrich us through knowing Him better and becoming more like Him; to this end He arranges our days with the proper mixture of joys and trials, gains and losses, pleasure and pain."

How often, in His gracious will, He lets us live in a well-watered land filled with opportunities, special surprises, rich relationships.

We're to receive these countless joys as love-gifts: "Lord, this shows what Your heart for me is like — You love to do things that delight me! Thank You!" The gifts, all of them, should draw us nearer to the Giver. We're to freely enjoy them, but not clutch them....

We're meant to kiss our joys, rather than clench them tightly and destroy them. Sometimes we turn our joys into trials by clinging to them too tightly.

—Ruth Myers in *THE PERFECT LOVE*

---

6. What blessings such as "opportunities, special surprises, rich relationships" are you especially enjoying in your life now?

7. In what important ways can you "kiss" these joys, rather than clenching tightly to them and destroying them?

Whatever He allows to touch our lives — seemingly good or bad — is an expression of His love and His desire for us. Whatever He permits or sends is an invitation to draw closer to Him.

—Ruth Myers in THE PERFECT LOVE

---

8. Is God currently allowing trials in your life as "an invitation to draw closer to Him"? If so, talk with God about these here, expressing your gratefulness for this expression of His love and desire for you.

9. Do you specifically see God's love portrayed in each of the following passages? If so, write a response to tell Him how you do, and how you feel about what you see.

a. James 1:2-4

b. Romans 8:28-29

c. Romans 5:3-5

In dealing with trials I've found it helpful to have my true
goals clearly set beforehand and to keep them in my
consciousness: to love God and know Him better, to be
conformed to Christ's image, to glorify Him and do His
will. Then when I feel disappointed or distressed, the
Lord can more quickly bring me back to this perspective:
"This trial comes to fulfill my chosen goals even though it
frustrates my surface desires. Therefore I welcome it."

—Ruth Myers in THE PERFECT LOVE

---

10. State here your true and most important goals in life,
remembering that God will even use trials in your life
to help you fulfill them.

Why not pause before the Lord and let Him search your
heart as you ask yourself, "Am I accepting my present
trials as steppingstones to a deeper knowledge of God's
love? Or am I resenting them, stumbling over them?"

—Ruth Myers in THE PERFECT LOVE

---

11. Ask yourself the questions suggested in the preceding quotation from *The Perfect Love*. Then answer them here:

12. Carefully write out **1 John 4:16** in the space below, then begin committing this passage to memory.

In time alone with God, review what you have written down and learned in this lesson.

Perhaps you sense something here that God wants you to especially understand and trust Him for at this time. If so, mark it in the lesson, then bring it again before the Lord in prayer and grateful praise.

Record here any further thoughts or prayer requests that come to your mind and heart.

So Vastly Wonderful

*A companion Bible study to Chapter 5
in THE PERFECT LOVE*

God already loves us perfectly, so we never have to try to
get Him to love us more!…

There's a reason God's love is perfect: It is linked
inseparably with everything He is.…

All of God's attributes are intertwined, and they all
undergird His personal, intimate, perfect love for you
and me.

—Ruth Myers in *THE PERFECT LOVE*

---

1. Use the truths in the following passages to help you
   offer God praise for His perfection.

   a. Deuteronomy 32:3-4

   b. Psalm 18:30

   c. Hebrews 7:26

d. 1 John 1:5

2. Meditate on Psalm 45:1-8, a prophetic foreshadowing of Christ our King. Record your thoughts here for each verse.

   a. Verse 1

   b. Verse 2

   c. Verse 3

   d. Verse 4

   e. Verse 5

   f. Verse 6

   g. Verse 7

h. Verse 8

There's another good reason to ponder deeply all of God's attributes: By doing so we learn more about ourselves....

Everything about *Him* reflects something about *me*....

—Ruth Myers in *THE PERFECT LOVE*

---

3. Look at the following passages. Because the God described in each verse is also *the God who personally loves you,* what conclusions can you make about why you can live your life with confidence?

   a. Psalm 42:8

   b. Psalm 57:10

   c. Psalm 86:5

   d. Psalm 89:14

   e. Psalm 103:8

Often I need Him to ride forth victoriously in my life because of an inner enemy that needs defeating — a fleshly attitude or desire — and He is more mighty than that inner enemy. Or I need Him to ride forth victoriously into circumstances with which I simply cannot cope or against some scheme or attack of Satan.

—Ruth Myers in *THE PERFECT LOVE*

4. Describe a recent or current situation that demonstrates your need for the Lord's victorious help and intervention.

5. What encouragement for your life do you find in the way God's character and help are described in Deuteronomy 33:26-29?

We need protection against the storms and battles of life, and against our spiritual enemy. We face temptations and struggles that we're not able to fight on our own. And God never intended for us to fight them on our own; He meant us to call upon our most mighty One and ask Him to ride forth victoriously to defeat what's wrong and defend what's right. So we ask Him, in His majesty, to do just that.

—Ruth Myers in *THE PERFECT LOVE*

6. What personal encouragement do you find in Psalm 66:3 in dealing with God's enemies (and yours)?

7. What encouragement for your life do you find in the way God's character and help are described in Psalm 68:4-10?

How easily we forget what a privilege it is to adore and worship God. How slow we sometimes are to realize that as we worship, we offer sacrifices of praise and thanksgiving that rejoice His heart. We give Him something unique, something no one else in the universe can give: our own personal love and adoration. This deepens the intimacy He longs for. It helps complete His joy in being our Father, our Beloved, our Friend, our Brother.

—Ruth Myers in *THE PERFECT LOVE*

8. Use any or all of the following passages to help you enjoy offering to God the personal love and adoration that can come only from you.

a. 1 Chronicles 29:11-12

b. Psalm 63:1

c. Psalm 97:3-5

d. Isaiah 57:15

e. Jeremiah 10:6-7

f. Jeremiah 32:17

g. Matthew 5:3

h. Ephesians 1:20-22

9. For helpful review, write out **1 John 4:16** from memory in the space below.

In time alone with God, review what you have written down and learned in this lesson.

Perhaps you sense something here that God wants you to especially understand and trust Him for at this time. If so, mark it in the lesson, then bring it again before the Lord in prayer and grateful praise.

Record here any further thoughts or prayer requests that come to your mind and heart.

So Perfectly My King

A companion Bible study to Chapter 6
in THE PERFECT LOVE

The choice is ours. We can try to guard and protect
ourselves, relying on our own puny defenses. Or we can
give up our "rights" and instead have this wonderful King
looking out for us, this Mighty One who always has our
best interests at heart.

The fact is, He Himself has promised to look out for
our rights.

—Ruth Myers in THE PERFECT LOVE

---

1. From each of the following passages, tell how God
   intends to "look out for our rights," and how He wants
   you to relate to Him.

   a. Psalm 37:5-11

   b. Psalm 143:8-12

   c. Isaiah 41:10-14

d. Isaiah 64:4

It's always God who's at the controls.... That circumstance in your life, which is causing you pain or dismay or
confusion or worse, is not accidental. As someone has
said, "With God nothing is accidental, nothing is
incidental, and no experience is wasted." God is working
for a purpose in allowing these things. He is looking out
for us, and He won't let anything happen to us that He
can't work together for our good, just as He has promised.

All this is far more than something to know; it's
something to praise Him for.

—Ruth Myers in *THE PERFECT LOVE*

---

2. Look in a fresh way at each of the following passages,
   and use them as a springboard for praising God for His
   sovereign control over everything that touches your
   life.

   a. Psalm 31:14-15

   b. Isaiah 46:9-10

   c. Daniel 4:34-35

d. Romans 11:36

We've been considering God's attributes, some of the
qualities we find in Him. We have seen that He is so
awesome and adequate: altogether desirable, perfect in
power and greatness, our Champion, the Blessed
Controller of all things, perfectly wise and good. Now the
question is, *What is God to me?* What are the various
relationships He has toward me that show me what to
expect of Him?

The most important truth in my life is that God wants
me to know Him in intimate, personal experience. Yes,
He wants me to know the true concepts about Him in
His Word. But He wants me to take each of those
concepts and allow Him to *be that to me* in personal
experience. If we want to be realists, if we want to live
realistically, we must know what God is and let Him be
that for us....

To really know God means that we see what He is in
relationship to us, and then more and more, in the
experiences of daily life, we let Him be that to us — *we
count on Him to be that.*

—Ruth Myers in *THE PERFECT LOVE*

---

3. Express in your own words these prayers of David:

a. Psalm 30:10

b. Psalm 31:2

4. In the following "I am" passages from the gospel of John, Jesus gives an image or statement about *what He is* to us. Respond to each one with written praise and thanksgiving in which you acknowledge in your own words, "Yes, Lord, You are that to me...."

a. 4:25-26

b. 6:35

c. 8:12

d. 10:7

e. 10:11

f. 11:25

g. 13:13

h. 14:6

i. 15:1

5. Carefully write out **Isaiah 41:13** in the space below, then begin committing this passage to memory.

In time alone with God, review what you have written down and learned in this lesson.

Perhaps you sense something here that God wants you to especially understand and trust Him for at this time. If so, mark it in the lesson, then bring it again before the Lord in prayer and grateful praise.

Record here any further thoughts or prayer requests that come to your mind and heart.

So Utterly and Completely Delightful

A companion Bible study to Chapter 7
in THE PERFECT LOVE

The tenacious love of God is both eternal and changeless.
These two concepts are wonderfully linked.

—Ruth Myers in THE PERFECT LOVE

---

1. How does God reveal to us that His love is both eternal
   and changeless? Use these passages to help you answer
   in a personal way:

   a. Deuteronomy 7:7-9

   b. Psalm 23:6

   c. Psalm 25:6

   d. Psalm 103:17

e. Psalm 136:1

f. Isaiah 54:10

Even when I'm letting something else be more important to me than God, God is still loving me. Even when He must discipline me, He says, "I won't go one bit farther than I have to for your good, and I would never cut you off from My love. My heart would never allow it." He recoils at the very thought of ever withdrawing His love for us....

As we're getting to know God's love we can be confident He'll never begin picking at us, He'll never start viewing us with a condemning, critical attitude. We can know that our personal beauty will continue to unfold before Him, to His delight.

—Ruth Myers in *THE PERFECT LOVE*

---

2. As a reading and study project, go through the following passages in Hosea and write your findings here about how this book reveals the Lord's unconditional love for His people. For each section of the book, summarize your most significant observations and impressions.

a. Hosea 1

b. Hosea 2

c. Hosea 3

d. Hosea 4–5

e. Hosea 6–7

f. Hosea 8–10

g. Hosea 11

h. Hosea 12–13

i. Hosea 14

God loves us far more than we know, and far more than we'll ever know. His love is so great that we'll never completely comprehend it.

This means there's always more about His love for us to discover and enjoy. What a privilege!

It also means we can always count on His love. It's always big enough to meet the deepest needs of our heart.

—Ruth Myers in *THE PERFECT LOVE*

3. Which of these passages help you most to comprehend the limitless love of God? Write a paraphrase of the passage you choose—Psalm 103:11, John 3:16, Romans 5:5-8, Ephesians 3:17-19, 1 John 3:1.

In no way do we ever need to earn God's love. He loves us — period. The flow of His love never stops. His love always shines forth undimmed. But our response determines whether it gets through to us. We can pull the blinds — or we can open them. We choose what we'll let ourselves be filled with, and God respects our choice. He does not force His love on us. But at all times His love flows and shines — perfect, unwavering, available to meet our needs.

—Ruth Myers in *THE PERFECT LOVE*

4. In what typical situations in your life are you most likely to "pull the blinds" on the constantly shining love of God?

> What qualifies us to receive God's love? We qualify simply
> because we need it.... To the person with desperate needs
> who is willing to admit them, God shows His love.
>
> —Ruth Myers in *THE PERFECT LOVE*

5. As you genuinely sense your own desperate needs, use
   the following passages to help you express this
   personally to God.

   a. Psalm 40:11-13,17

   b. Psalm 51:1-6

   c. Psalm 94:17-19

> He is immeasurably generous. His love gives and gives
> and is never depleted, because His power and resources
> are unlimited. He never has need to give in a grudging
> way....
>
> God delights to do the things that delight us, and so
> He gives to us lavishly.... He is not a stingy God.
>
> —Ruth Myers in *THE PERFECT LOVE*

6. What do you see in these passages that helps convince
   you that God's love is lavish, and never grudging or

stingy? Express your gratefulness and praise for the richness you find here.

a. Romans 5:17

b. 2 Corinthians 8:9

c. Ephesians 1:5-8

d. Ephesians 2:4-5

e. Ephesians 3:20

f. 2 Peter 1:3

7. For helpful review, write out **Isaiah 41:13** from memory in the space below.

In time alone with God, review what you have written down and learned in this lesson.

Perhaps you sense something here that God wants you to especially understand and trust Him for at this time. If so, mark it in the lesson, then bring it again before the Lord in prayer and grateful praise.

Record here any further thoughts or prayer requests that come to your mind and heart.

Our Priceless Privilege

A companion Bible study to Chapter 8
in THE PERFECT LOVE

We've looked closely — perhaps more closely than you
ever have before — at what God's love is like, this
beautiful, vast ocean of delight. But how can we learn to
swim in it, to relax and enjoy the feel of it?

—Ruth Myers in *THE PERFECT LOVE*

---

1. What do you think is the best answer (for you
personally) to the above question?

The highest privilege life can offer is to know God and
become more intimately acquainted with Him, an
acquaintance made possible through knowing His Son,
Jesus Christ....

I wonder: What is your chief pursuit in life? What do
you really want?

> What do you actually *demand* from life? What comes
> to mind when you think, "I must have this"?
>
> —Ruth Myers in *THE PERFECT LOVE*

2. Answer here as thoroughly as you can the questions
   listed in the preceding selection from *The Perfect Love*.

> The more personally we take the messages of God's love,
> the more His love will change our lives. In fact, it's
> impossible for me to take God *too* personally. He actually
> wants me to take His love very seriously. He longs for me
> to experience Himself and His love, and He wants my
> experience of Him to constantly grow more rich and full.
>
> —Ruth Myers in *THE PERFECT LOVE*

3. Respond in a personal way to the truths in each of the
   following passages. Remind yourself to take each truth
   personally.

   a. Psalm 27:8

b. Psalm 73:25-26

c. Jeremiah 29:13

d. Hebrews 11:6

e. Hebrews 12:22-23

f. Hebrews 12:28

We ourselves determine whether or not we experience a truly intimate and life-changing relationship with Him. If we respond to Him, His love is powerful and transforming. It cannot help but revolutionize our lives in a phenomenal way.

—Ruth Myers in *THE PERFECT LOVE*

---

4. Look in a fresh way at 2 Corinthians 5:17. What new meaning does this truth have for you now in light of what you've recently been learning about God's love?

5. In an earlier lesson we looked at five love-gifts God provides to help us draw nearer to Him. The fifth of these love-gifts is the path of obedience. Using the following passages, describe what this path of obedience means personally to you in your relationship with the Lord, and what you can expect it to mean in the degree of your experience of His love.

a. Deuteronomy 7:9

b. Psalm 25:10

c. Psalm 119:88

d. Psalm 119:124

e. John 14:21

f. 1 John 2:3-6

Have you honestly come to the conclusion that you cannot find true satisfaction apart from Him, and therefore you won't even try?...

Is our desire to know Him strong enough so that we can tell Him honestly, "At any cost, dear Lord, by any road — and through any circumstances You want to use in my life"? Do you want to know Him that badly?

—Ruth Myers in *The Perfect Love*

6. Record here your personal response to the questions in the preceding selection from *The Perfect Love*.

Why not pause now and ask the Lord for five things: (1) that you will spend more time in His Word, seeking to know Him better; (2) that the Holy Spirit will increasingly fill and control you and flood your heart with God's love; (3) that, as a member of Christ's body, you will take full advantage of your opportunities to experience and express God's love; (4) that you will receive each of life's circumstances as love-gifts from Him, and (5) that you will constantly choose the path of obedience, where you'll enjoy His love more and more.

—Ruth Myers in THE PERFECT LOVE

7. Write here your personal prayer in which you ask the Lord for the five things listed in the preceding quotation from *The Perfect Love.*

A relationship with God (like any close relationship) takes time and teamwork. It won't become deep if we are distracted or indifferent or erect barriers. It takes the willingness to bare our souls and pour out our heart to Him. As in human relationships, it takes time to really listen, to develop trust in the other person, then to learn to trust him or her still more....

There is no other way. *I must take time to enjoy Him and let Him love me.*

Are you taking enough time? Most of us must consistently prune back other activities to truly have enough time for Him. What pruning have you already done? Is there more you need to consider?

—Ruth Myers in THE PERFECT LOVE

---

8. Answer here the questions in the above selection from *The Perfect Love*.

And have you learned the value of setting aside half a day every month or so for a date with God, an extended time of prayer and meditation on His Word? If not, plan ahead for it and put it on your calendar.

—Ruth Myers in THE PERFECT LOVE

---

9. Record here your response to the above question and suggestion from *The Perfect Love*. (Write your plans here for your next special half-day with God.)

Our heavenly Father does not expect us to do everything perfectly. Even at our best we've still got our dirty thumbs in the glass. That's true in all our service. We'll serve Him perfectly in heaven, but never here. But God understands. He accepts imperfect service because it's a love relationship. He's a Father who's delighted that we love Him and want to please Him.

—Ruth Myers in *THE PERFECT LOVE*

10. What does God remember about us, according to Psalm 103:13-14?

Something else is just as important as reserving the right amount of time for seeking God. That is having the right mindset — or perhaps we should call it "heart-set" or even "life-set," since it involves more than just a way of thinking. It's closely related to our emotional life. It means being honest before God, accepting both our overall inherent weakness as well as all our separate little weaknesses, and pouring out our hearts before Him. But it's also a commitment to pursuing Him, a commitment we can maintain even when our feelings don't agree. Because it's the basic bent of our heart, we can go back to it and be firmly anchored in it, in spite of what our feelings may be telling us.

Most of all it's an openness. It's being receptive toward God. We open our inner eyes and turn them to Him. We see who He is, let our hearts drink it in, and then let Him be to us what we need as the hours go by.

So our part is to need and receive.

—Ruth Myers in THE PERFECT LOVE

11. How would you describe your "heart-set" or "life-set" for seeking God? How open are you, really? How receptive are you? Talk about this with the Lord, and record your thoughts here.

And I wonder: As He bestows His gifts, do we with gratefulness turn to Him and let Him be central in our joys so that they cement our heart closer to His?... How often do we let God's blessings become more important to us than He Himself is?

—Ruth Myers in THE PERFECT LOVE

12. How would you answer the above questions from The Perfect Love?

My final suggestion to you in this chapter is to pore over
the Scriptures on God's love that really mean something
to you, the passages in which your heart has truly heard
God's voice and recognized His love. Soak in them
awhile. Go back to them often. Memorize them, think
about their meaning, let the Holy Spirit grip you deeply
inside with their truth. Then you can return to them
again and again to find rescue and enrichment.

—Ruth Myers in THE PERFECT LOVE

13. Make a list here of Scriptures that communicate the
most to you about God's love.

14. Carefully write out **Psalm 108:4** in the space below,
then begin committing this passage to memory.

In time alone with God, review what you have written down and learned in this lesson.

Perhaps you sense something here that God wants you to especially understand and trust Him for at this time. If so, mark it in the lesson, then bring it again before the Lord in prayer and grateful praise.

Record here any further thoughts or prayer requests that come to your mind and heart.

~

The Power
of His Perfect Love

*A companion Bible study to Chapter 9
in THE PERFECT LOVE*

"God is not in the business of condemning His children."
Now that's good news. But how can God refrain from
condemning me, with my assortment of besetting sins?…
How can a righteous God say to me, "You're not
condemned"?

He can say this because when Jesus died on the cross,
He paid for all my sin. He bore all the guilt of my whole
life — past, present and future….

Therefore if we have trusted Christ, all the guilt and
condemnation of our sin has been removed. Even when
we sin now, the condemnation is not placed back on us,
for God would not be fair if He required the condemnation twice. So what happens when we sin? Our
fellowship with God is broken, so sooner or later our
peace is disturbed and our joy evaporates. But we're still
His children. And God never condemns us because He is
just and the penalty has been paid in full.

—Ruth Myers in *THE PERFECT LOVE*

---

1. What do the following passages teach us about our
   freedom from God's condemnation?

a. Psalm 130:3-4

b. Isaiah 53:6

c. John 5:24

d. Romans 4:8

e. Romans 5:1

f. Romans 8:1

g. Romans 8:33-34

h. Galatians 3:13

Some see a danger in teaching such total forgiveness. They're afraid people will think they're free to do anything they want, and then come back and receive automatic forgiveness just by saying, "Please forgive me." Then it's back to sinning again.

But it doesn't work that way because God has given us a new life that can never again be happy in sin.... If we have no desire to please our Father and avoid sin, we do well to examine ourselves and make sure we really belong to Christ (2 Corinthians 13:5).

—Ruth Myers in *THE PERFECT LOVE*

2. What danger, if any, do you see in the teaching of total forgiveness? How can this danger be avoided in a biblical way? (Explain your answer.)

We must let this truth grip our hearts, for we live like the person we see ourselves to be. The more we realize who we are in Christ, the more we can live according to the new image of ourselves that we carry around within us. If we still carry within ourselves a basic image of being guilty and condemned and enslaved to sin, we'll be far more prone to live fleshly lives. We'll be much more likely to give in to sin. And we won't attract others to this wonderful person Jesus. But as we allow the Lord, through the Scriptures, to engrave on our hearts who we really are in Christ...we can live like kings and queens.

—Ruth Myers in THE PERFECT LOVE

3. How would you describe your essential self-image, especially as it regards your relationship with God? (Answer as thoroughly as you can.)

4. What impact on your self-image should the truth in these passages have? Think about each one in a fresh way. (You may want to express your answer in words of gratitude to God for these truths.)

a. Romans 6:11-14

b. Philippians 2:13

c. Colossians 2:13-14

d. Hebrews 4:15-16

God loves to forgive us. When we make this about-face
from our sin and turn to Him, He welcomes us fervently
just as the prodigal son's father welcomed him....

He is never reluctant to forgive. He always accepts us
as persons, as dearly loved children, regardless of how
strongly He hates and rejects our sin — an important
distinction to make.

—Ruth Myers in *THE PERFECT LOVE*

---

5. In each of these passages, in what ways can you truly
   see that God loves to forgive us?

   a. Psalm 32:5

   b. Proverbs 28:13

   c. Matthew 26:27-28

   d. Mark 2:1-12

e. Luke 23:34

f. Ephesians 1:7

g. 1 John 1:9

h. 1 John 2:1

6. Review the story of the prodigal son beginning in Luke
   15:11. What important insights come to you as you
   read this story and think about God's love?

The entire Trinity — the Father and Son and Holy
Spirit — is involved in giving us this privilege of not only
being forgiven but also feeling forgiven. All three are
involved in ensuring us a life that is liberated, confident,
conquering, and increasingly conformed to the image of
Christ.

—Ruth Myers in THE PERFECT LOVE

7. For each of these passages, record your personal
   responses to the truth about God the Father's
   involvement in your forgiveness:

   a. Lamentations 3:22-23

   b. Exodus 34:6-7

   c. Hebrews 10:16-17

8. For the following passages, record your personal
   responses to the truth about Jesus Christ's involvement
   in your forgiveness:

   a. Hebrews 2:17

b. Hebrews 7:24-25

c. Hebrews 10:14

The Holy Spirit uses the Word of God to wash our feet day by day, to cleanse us. The Bible compares both the Word and the Spirit to water (John 7:37-39, Ephesians 5:26). And water of course has great cleansing power. As we have seen, we who know Christ are completely clean through our new birth — we never need to repeat that. Now it's just the "dirt that soils our feet" as we walk through life that needs to be washed away day by day. The Holy Spirit by His mercy does this for us. How often do you praise God for this wonderful cleansing?

—Ruth Myers in *THE PERFECT LOVE*

---

9. For these passages, record your personal responses to the truth about the Holy Spirit's involvement in your forgiveness:

a. John 16:8-10

b. Ephesians 4:30

c. Titus 3:5

10. For helpful review, write out **Psalm 108:4** from memory in the space below.

In time alone with God, review what you have written down and learned in this lesson.

Perhaps you sense something here that God wants you to especially understand and trust Him for at this time. If so, mark it in the lesson, then bring it again before the Lord in prayer and grateful praise.

Record here any further thoughts or prayer requests that come to your mind and heart.

In His Perfect Love, I'm Truly Alive

A companion Bible study to Chapter 10
in THE PERFECT LOVE

This chapter, perhaps more than all the others, covers truths that are ultra-vital for a life that pleases God and brings consistent enjoyment of His love. These are truths that we cannot possibly grasp unless the Holy Spirit opens our eyes in a special way. There's no way we can wrap our natural minds around them....

And I encourage you to plead with God for fresh, clear understanding of these truths. Pause now and pray that these truths will dawn like a fresh and beautiful sunrise in your heart. If the Lord has already done this for you, pray that you will experience the reality of these truths with greater constancy.

—Ruth Myers in *THE PERFECT LOVE*

---

1. Record your own prayer here, following the above suggestions.

> "It's not only true that my life is Christ's, but my life is
> Christ."… This truth that Christ is my life became a light
> within me — and what a difference it made!
>
> Now I could grasp the meaning of those words in
> Colossians 3:4, "Christ who is our life." And I was able to
> personalize this truth: "Christ is *my* life."
>
> —Ruth Myers in *THE PERFECT LOVE*

2. How do the following passages show that *Christ is your life?* In your answer, respond to each passage by personalizing the truth you see there.

a. John 15:5

b. Romans 8:10

c. Colossians 1:17

> As believers whom God has made righteous, we have the
> actual life of Jesus in the core of our being….
>
> This is the real me now. This is my new identity, my
> true identity. Sin is still in me, but it's not a valid part of
> me; it is no longer my nature or my master. Sin still tries
> to pose as part of me, as my partner and "friend." But sin

is actually a traitor in the camp and a liar. It is no longer part of the true me. Deep inside me, I've become a totally new person with Christ and His life in me.

—Ruth Myers in *THE PERFECT LOVE*

3. How do these passages reinforce the truth that you are a totally new person with Christ and His life inside you? (You may want to express your answer in words of gratitude to God for these truths.)

   a. John 1:12-13

   b. Colossians 1:21-22

In our lives, the Cross and the empty tomb form a dividing line. That line separates the Death side from the Life side.

On the Death side is spiritual death.... Guilt and condemnation belong on this side where Satan and our flesh like to keep us in our experience.

But the right side of the dividing line is the Life side, the God side. On this side is spiritual life, total forgiveness, and freedom. Strength and vitality come to us here because we're alive with His life. This is possible only because, through faith, we've been given a share in Christ's death and in His resurrection.

—Ruth Myers in *THE PERFECT LOVE*

4. Draw a simple diagram here showing the "Death side" and "Life side" of your life, with the Cross and the empty tomb as a dividing line. Add labels or pictures that show something of what each side of that line has represented in your life.

Indwelling sin is like an ugly, smelly garbage can. Lots of obnoxious things come out of it — things like immorality, hostility that hasn't been dealt with, anger that's been handled wrongly, anxiety that we haven't renounced, plus envy, resentment, bitterness, self-condemnation, and the fear that deafens us to God's "Be not afraid." Each of us has our own assortment of sins that most often shift our experience back to the garbage-pail side. And the most basic sin for all of us is failure to trust God and count on what He says in His Word about Himself, about us, and about how life runs well.

The left side of the Cross is what I experience whenever I sin, before I repent and confess and receive the Lord's fresh forgiveness. After being forgiven, I can return in my actual experience to my new identity on the right side of the Cross.

—Ruth Myers in *THE PERFECT LOVE*

5. What do these passages tell us about the "Death side" of our lives?

   a. 1 Corinthians 6:9-11

   b. Galatians 5:19

   c. Ephesians 4:31

   d. Colossians 3:5

6. What do these passages tell us about the "Life side" of our lives?

   a. Romans 6:4,11

   b. Romans 8:11

c. 1 Corinthians 6:17

d. 2 Corinthians 3:18

e. Colossians 3:3-4

f. 1 John 5:11-13

We need to ask ourselves, "Which side am I identifying with? Where am I choosing to live? And when my fleshly ways take over, how quickly do I use the lid of truth — Spirit-empowered truth — to put a stop to their outflow?... Where do I choose to live this moment, this hour, this day?"

—Ruth Myers in *THE PERFECT LOVE*

---

7. Answer here the questions in the above selection from *The Perfect Love.*

> We have the opportunity every morning, by faith, to mentally put on our robe of Christ's righteousness. It is already in us, but we can decide consciously to remember this with joy and choose to "wear" it in our attitudes and actions.
>
> —Ruth Myers in *THE PERFECT LOVE*

8. How do the passages below reinforce the concept of mentally putting on our robe of Christ's righteousness?

   a. Isaiah 61:10

   b. Romans 13:14

   c. Galatians 3:27

   d. Ephesians 4:22-24

> We can exult in the fact that He has given us His glorious righteousness, has made it an actual part of who we are. We can thank Him that growing in righteousness is

letting the reality of who we are shine out more and more. It is simply learning to be ourselves, our new selves, to His glory as our Maker and our Father.

Isn't it wonderful that God has actually given us *His* righteousness! It's not that He looks at us through Jesus-colored glasses so that He doesn't really see us, but only Jesus. No, we actually have His righteousness imparted to us so that we can say, "I *am* righteous, in my true self, in the core of my being. My spirit has been united with His Spirit, and I'm righteous."

—Ruth Myers in THE PERFECT LOVE

---

9. Knowing that *Christ's* righteousness is now your righteousness—record your heart-responses to the truths about righteousness in the following passages.

a. Romans 6:13,18

b. Romans 14:17

c. 1 Corinthians 1:30

d. 2 Corinthians 5:21

e. Ephesians 6:14

f. James 5:16

Ever since the Holy Spirit came to dwell in us, our inner
being has been permanently linked with the vast reservoir
of the living God, with its continual, inexhaustible supply
of fresh, life-enhancing water. As we simply yield to the
indwelling Spirit, His life springs up in us in a refreshing,
invigorating way. It's a bit like children running through a
lawn sprinkler on a sweltering day, except that it's inward
and spiritual. Or it's like watering plants that are wilted
and drooping, then watching them perk up. But we don't
have to wait until we're wilted, depleted, or dying of
thirst. The flow can be continual as we count on the Life ·
within us, letting the Spirit of God revive us and give us
freshness, enthusiasm, and vigor.

—Ruth Myers in *THE PERFECT LOVE*

---

10. In *The Perfect Love* the author writes of being taught
    about "several stages that we typically go through in
    our growing consciousness of our relationship with
    God." She describes them this way:

    > In the first stage we realize that we have a Father in
    > heaven. As new Christians we recognize with excite-
    > ment, "I'm a child of God. This wonderful, exalted
    > God is up there with all His love and power caring
    > for me, watching over me, and listening to my
    > prayers."...
    >   In the second stage we realize, "God is not only
    > in heaven, He's also beside me. He comforts and
    > guides me as my Shepherd. He is my Friend to com-
    > municate with, and my Beloved who holds my right
    > hand and says to me, 'Fear not, I will help you.'"...
    >   In the third stage we move even closer to God in

our experience. We realize, "He is also living in me. He's not only with me out there as my daily Guide and Helper, but He's indwelling me, closer than any human relationship can ever be."

And that's wonderful. But even that falls short of the fourth stage, where it dawns on us that we have an inner union with Him. We realize, "His Spirit is dwelling in my spirit in an intermingled way. Amazing!"

Is your own spiritual growth reflected in this process of four stages? If so, explain here the stages you have experienced.

In our new life we have all that it takes to love God and to love others, and that's the heartbeat of true Christlikeness.

—Ruth Myers in *The Perfect Love*

---

11. Take a personal look at Ephesians 5:1-2. What will make it possible for you to obey what God commands us to do in these verses?

12. Carefully write out **Psalm 100:5** in the space below, then begin committing this passage to memory.

In time alone with God, review what you have written down and learned in this lesson.

Perhaps you sense something here that God wants you to especially understand and trust Him for at this time. If so, mark it in the lesson, then bring it again before the Lord in prayer and grateful praise.

Record here any further thoughts or prayer requests that come to your mind and heart.

~

In His Perfect Love,
I'm Truly Free

A companion Bible study to Chapter 11
in THE PERFECT LOVE

True freedom comes when we give up the false freedom of
our fleshly independence and submit to "captivity" under
God — captivity to His perfect love.

—Ruth Myers in THE PERFECT LOVE

---

1. Read the words of Jesus in the following passages.
   Summarize here *what* Jesus said. Then explain how it
   relates personally to you.

   a. Luke 4:18

   b. John 8:31-32, 36

Do we compare ourselves with others, face or fear disapproval, become discouraged at our weaknesses and sins? Our loving King is not comparing.... He does not condemn, blame, or exclude any of us. His favor is constant. It neither increases when we excel nor lessens when we fail. It shines into our lives as we let it in.

Why then should anxieties keep us awake at night? Why do we ever waste time blaming others, reproaching ourselves, thinking of excuses? These are symptoms of unbelief — of relying on something other than God's grace.

—Ruth Myers in *THE PERFECT LOVE*

2. Have you recently experienced any of the following situations? If so, carefully and prayerfully think about it, and ask yourself, "What was I relying on instead of God's grace?" Record your thoughts here.

a. Comparing yourself with others.

b. Facing or fearing disapproval from others.

c. Becoming discouraged at your weaknesses and sins.

d. Being kept awake at night by anxieties.

Again and again through the years, truths from God's Word have helped dispel false beliefs and thought patterns that would sidetrack me and destroy my peace. But about six or seven years ago, the Lord prodded me to start a more intensive search for any thoughts and emotions He wanted me to deal with in a new way. So I began to pray, "Lord, is there anything in me that hinders my walk with You? Any false thoughts about You or about myself that keep me from fully doing Your will? Any hurts or griefs that I've never faced head-on, pouring out my heart before You and letting You heal and comfort? Any areas where I still operate independently, relying on my own strength and my own ways of handling life? Any false beliefs I've never clearly renounced? I don't want any area of my life to be walled off to You!"

—Ruth Myers in THE PERFECT LOVE

3. Look again at the questions asked in the author's prayer quoted above. Ask them about yourself as you bring these same questions before God in prayer. Then record here your thoughts as you listen for His answers.

Whether or not I feel the reality of His working at any given moment, I'm to proceed by faith, choosing to trust Him to work in me and along with me. Then I'm to assume my responsibility to do His will: "His will — nothing more, nothing less, nothing else."

His part and ours — where does one end, the other begin? We cannot tell, for they inseparably interact. In response to His working we choose to work and to rely on Him, and then He works in new ways.

—Ruth Myers in THE PERFECT LOVE

4. Keep in mind the freedom God wants you to experience as you study the following passages. Then summarize the truths they contain under the appropriate categories below. Psalms 46:10, 68:19-20, and 103:1-5; Proverbs 4:23; Isaiah 40:31; Philippians 4:6-8; Colossians 1:29; Hebrews 3:14; and 1 John 5:14.

MY PART   HIS PART

When things go wrong, how do we react? Some of us
tend to withdraw into silence.... Others of us would
never withdraw; we're quick to speak up or act in an
unwise way. And some of us alternate between those two
reactions, sometimes withdrawing, and sometimes acting
or speaking unwisely and in haste.

God delivers us from both these wrong reactions, for
in His Word He has given us behavior patterns for how to
cope with life's difficulties in appropriate, godly ways.

—Ruth Myers in THE PERFECT LOVE

5. How *do* you typically react when things go wrong?

6. From what you know of God's Word, how would you
   summarize the "appropriate, godly ways" in which He
   wants us to cope with life's difficulties? (Remember to
   build your answer on biblical truth, not on human
   opinion.)

Only God's perfect love can deliver us from our inability
to love others. How often have you been frustrated
because you were unable to love family members or

friends as perfectly as you wanted? Occasionally something comes out of you that is just the opposite of how you really feel. You know you're supposed to love them, yet in little ways here and there you find yourself hurting them instead. But as we more and more embrace and rest in God's love for us, the experience of that love empowers us to more freely channel it to others.

—Ruth Myers in *THE PERFECT LOVE*

7. Have you recently been frustrated in not being able to love family members or friends as perfectly as you wanted?

If your answer is yes, look back over your written responses in earlier lessons in this book. In what specific ways do you believe your stronger embrace of God's love will help you experience more perfect love for others?

8. For helpful review, write out **Psalm 100:5** from memory in the space below.

In time alone with God, review what you have written down and learned in this lesson.

Perhaps you sense something here that God wants you to especially understand and trust Him for at this time. If so, mark it in the lesson, then bring it again before the Lord in prayer and grateful praise.

Record here any further thoughts or prayer requests that come to your mind and heart.

~

In His Perfect Love, I Am Secure

A companion Bible study to Chapter 12 in THE PERFECT LOVE

Just as we use a mirror to see that we look all right physically, so we also use mirrors to find out if we're all right as persons. Emotionally, spiritually, and psychologically we need a mirror in which to see what we're like.

The mirror people most often depend on is the mirror of other people's responses.

—Ruth Myers in *THE PERFECT LOVE*

---

1. In what ways have you found yourself depending at times on the mirror of other people's responses?

It's been said that every problem we face, either within our personalities or in our relationships, can somehow be traced to a false sense of identity or a lack of inner sureness about who we are. In my life, at least, this tends to be true....

Whatever our age, our basic needs are the same: We require the confidence, inner sureness, and security that only perfect love can give. We need an acceptable image of ourselves — a sense of worth, of belonging, and of competence. There's nothing wrong with needing and wanting what we might call ego support — but there is something wrong with seeking it apart from God.

—Ruth Myers in THE PERFECT LOVE

2. Let your heart soak in the truths of the following verses, as you look to the Lord for your sense of identity, your inner sureness, your sense of worth and of belonging and of competence.

   Write down your personal response to the truth in each passage.

   a. Psalm 5:11-12

   b. Psalm 16:2

   c. Psalm 32:10

   d. Psalm 91:1

   e. Romans 8:38-39

We look to others for approval and identity support in three basic ways — through our appearance, our performance, and our status.

First let's consider appearance — how good we look....

Does it bother us when we can't afford some of the clothes that are "in"? Or when someone hints that we've gained a few pounds or gray hairs or wrinkles, and this doesn't fit with the image we're trying to project? How long does such a remark disturb us? Or if someone compliments our appearance, how long afterward do we keep replaying their words in our mind? It's fine to be pleased with compliments and to give them; the Bible gives many examples of encouraging others and commending them for how well they're doing. And being human, we're bound to be bothered at times by disapproval. But how quickly do we get back to the firm foundation of what God thinks about us?

—Ruth Myers in THE PERFECT LOVE

3. Answer here, as thoroughly and honestly as you can, the questions about your *appearance* in the above selection from *The Perfect Love*.

Then there's performance — how well we do. We want to be a success in something. It's not wrong to work hard and perform well, but *why* do we want to succeed? Do we want to be known as a skillful teacher or manager or salesperson or workman or entrepreneur? Or as a successful parent?... Do we want others to see us as an effective communicator, a proven leader, an expert organizer? Even as a faithful Christian? Is it because we're trying to gain people's approval, instead of resting in God's love and approval for our inner support? Do we seek to do our best in order to build a reputation — or in order to please and honor God?

—Ruth Myers in THE PERFECT LOVE

4. Answer the questions about your *performance* in the above selection from *The Perfect Love*.

There's also status — how important we are. Are we a bit too pleased when others call attention to our promotions or possessions or achievements — even our effectiveness in serving the Lord, or our golden opportunities — anything that makes us appear more important than others?

—Ruth Myers in THE PERFECT LOVE

5. Answer the question about your *status* in the above selection from *The Perfect Love*.

Whoever or whatever supports us inside is our god. That's one of the functions of a god. So ask yourself: Who or what do I depend on for my inner support? Who is on my throne of my life? Is it myself? Is it something or someone else — anything or anyone other than God?

Who or what am I trusting? Is it my ability to look good? My ability to perform? Or the status I can muster through the person I marry, or my family's prominence, or my education, or my personal success, or whatever?

—Ruth Myers in *THE PERFECT LOVE*

6. Ask yourself the questions in the above selection from *The Perfect Love,* and record your honest answers here.

Each of us who believes in Jesus has come into real, living contact with the one true mirror, the mirror of God's love. This mirror always reflects genuine acceptance and a totally accurate picture of who we are. It shows us wonderful, uplifting truths about how acceptable we are in Christ and how much God values the unique person He has created each of us to be.... The more personally we embrace this picture, the more it gives us a profound sense of being accepted and secure in spite of being far from perfect.

—Ruth Myers in *THE PERFECT LOVE*

Jesus asked in John 5:44, "How can you believe, who receive honor from one another, and do not seek the honor that comes from the only God?" (NKJV). Seeking approval and praise anywhere but from God is an obstacle to faith. Have you ever tried to trust Him more and can't? Have you felt you'd like to have more faith, but it just doesn't seem to come? You claim this or that promise, but can't really believe it? You read what God says about Himself and about you, but you can't seem to lay hold on it with a steady faith?

How can you believe if you're reverting to the worldly system of trying to gain honor from other people? There's nothing wrong with seeking honor, as long as we seek the honor and praise that comes from God alone. And we do this by living for His glory in people's eyes, not for our own.

—Ruth Myers in *THE PERFECT LOVE*

7. After careful reflection, list here some important, practical ways in which you can live for God's glory in the eyes of others, rather than for your own glory.

God…is a master at telling us positive, even glorious truths about who we are. The more we let these in, the more we'll be able to build up others rather than tear them down.

Are we really secure in God's love because we truly understand our identity in Christ? If so, that security will especially work itself out in how we relate to others.

—Ruth Myers in THE PERFECT LOVE

8. As you better understand your identity in Christ while you grow more secure in God's love, who are the people in your life who will benefit most as that security works itself out in your relationships? List their names here. Beside each name, write down something practical you can do to build up that person in some way.

9. Carefully write out **Psalm 84:11** in the space below, then begin committing this passage to memory.

In time alone with God, review what you have written down and learned in this lesson.

Perhaps you sense something here that God wants you to especially understand and trust Him for at this time. If so, mark it in the lesson, then bring it again before the Lord in prayer and grateful praise.

Record here any further thoughts or prayer requests that come to your mind and heart.

~

In His Perfect Love, I Am Significant

A companion Bible study to Chapter 13
in THE PERFECT LOVE

In His perfect love I'm freed from purposelessness and the fear of insignificance.

This is one of the big problems of modern living: Why am I here? People look and look, but fail to find a purpose big enough to really challenge them and keep them from being disappointed and frustrated with life. They try something new that promises purpose, then it fizzles out and they feel bored and purposeless again. God created us first of all for a loving, intimate relationship with Him, so we'll always be empty until we find that. Our chief reason for being is to glorify God and enjoy Him forever. But we cannot find that enjoyment until we begin to know Him better and to grasp His love more fully.

—Ruth Myers in *THE PERFECT LOVE*

---

1. Read what David prays in Psalm 39:4-7. Then in your own words and from your own heart, talk with God about these same issues, and record your prayer here.

God has two primary purposes in this world around which I think all His other purposes revolve. First of all He is at work here and now to call out from this fallen world "a people for His name" (Acts 15:14, NKJV) — a people for Himself who will believe in Him and let Him be their Savio and Lord.

Second, He plans "to bring many sons [and daughters!] to glory" (Hebrews 2:10). This does not mean simply transporting us physically up to heaven. It means that He will change us into glorious people, conformed to Christ's image. We'll be part of His vast family of sons and daughters who all reflect without fault or blemish the glorious excellencies of Christ....

God is looking forward to that even more than we are, and His plan for now is to put disciples of Christ everywhere, disciples who will follow Him ever more closely and honor Him ever more fully.

This is His purpose, and we have a part. What tremendous significance He bestows on us!

—Ruth Myers in *THE PERFECT LOVE*

2. How would you describe *your* part in God's primary purposes for this world?

> God also gives me the significance of simply channeling
> His perfect love to others.
>
> —Ruth Myers in *THE PERFECT LOVE*

3. Who are the most important people to whom God has given you the significant task of channeling His perfect love? Record their names here, and use this moment as an opportunity to pray for each person.

> God, in His beautiful love, also gives us the priceless
> significance and privilege of being His witnesses.
>
> —Ruth Myers in *THE PERFECT LOVE*

4. Write here the names of non-Christians for whom you are praying, and to whom your life and your words can be a witness for Christ. Use this moment as an opportunity to pray for each person.

> We must keep our priorities straight because God has
> given each of us certain core roles. He has assigned us
> certain basic responsibilities appropriate for the privileged
> position He called us to in our relationships with others,
> especially in the family.
>
> —Ruth Myers in *THE PERFECT LOVE*

5. What are your God-given core roles?

> God, in His gracious and wise love, helps us focus on our
> eternal significance by teaching us how to hope.
>
> —Ruth Myers in *THE PERFECT LOVE*

6. Allow your meditation on the following passages to
   help you rejoice in the true hope God has given you.
   Record your thoughts here.

   a. Romans 8:18

   b. 1 Corinthians 15:42-44

c. 1 Corinthians 15:51-57

d. 1 Peter 1:6-8

e. 1 Peter 4:13

As He calls us home when we die or when Christ returns,
it will be glorious for us all — breathtaking, unimag-
inable splendor. And each of us will hear and know His
personal greeting, "Welcome, My beloved child."

But not all of us will hear His "Well done, good and
faithful servant."

The splendid, breathtaking wonder for all, and His
warm welcome for all — but His "Well done" only for
some.

I deeply desire to hear both greetings — don't you?...

If we do what He asks, He'll reward us for keeping our
priorities straight and persisting in doing His will. And
He'll say, "Well done, good and faithful servant." How I
want to hear that!

—Ruth Myers in *THE PERFECT LOVE*

---

7. How strongly do you wish to hear Jesus say, "Well done, good and faithful servant," at the end of your earthly life? Consider this carefully, and record here your thoughts and words of prayer.

8. For helpful review, write out **Psalm 84:11** from memory in the space below.

In time alone with God, review what you have written down and learned in this lesson.

Perhaps you sense something here that God wants you to especially understand and trust Him for at this time. If so, mark it in the lesson, then bring it again before the Lord in prayer and grateful praise.

Record here any further thoughts or prayer requests that come to your mind and heart.

~

In His Perfect Love, I Am Honored and Satisfied

A companion Bible study to Chapters 14 and 15 in THE PERFECT LOVE

You and I, wherever we are, share the honored position of being seated with Christ. We share His authority over Satan and his helpers, and His dominion over all things. By His grace we can reign in our actual daily lives now.

—Ruth Myers in THE PERFECT LOVE

---

1. Record here your meditations on the following verses, as you thank God for the honored position He has given you in Christ.

   a. 1 Peter 2:9

   b. 1 Thessalonians 1:4

   c. Colossians 3:1-2

d. Colossians 2:10

e. Ephesians 2:6-7

f. Romans 8:35-37

g. Romans 8:30

h. Matthew 11:11

i. Isaiah 43:4

Yet I wonder if we really look upon ourselves as highly privileged individuals? As raised-up ones with Christ? As highly favored by the high King of heaven who is predisposed to look upon us with favor at all times because we're united to His Son? As highly honored?

Do people looking at our lives get a sense that we're overwhelmed by God's favor, that we live in the light of the high privileges we have in Christ?

This is our identity, our true standing — so why do we so often live like deprived persons, like beggars?

—Ruth Myers in THE PERFECT LOVE

2. What are your personal answers to the questions asked in the above selection from *The Perfect Love?*

We are not deprived persons, and God doesn't want us to live as though we were.

—Ruth Myers in THE PERFECT LOVE

3. What scriptural truths convince you that the above statement from *The Perfect Love* is true, or not true?

Our God of intensely personal, overflowing love has given us Himself as our share in life. He is the source of all good things, the all-sufficient God who is enough. He satisfies us with a beautiful part in life, a pleasant share.

Yet with reflection you and I may discern areas in our lives where we lack satisfaction and character growth. If that's true for you, I urge you to take time to think about this. Write down these areas, then bring the list before God. Tell Him that you keep having trouble with this temptation or in that relationship, or with this or that responsibility or circumstance. Then pray, "Now, Lord, show me the cure," and await His answer. Bring your request to Him time after time. Spend time in His Word, time enough for Him to both examine your heart and express His love. Gradually find in the Scriptures a "handle" for each need or problem that concerns you — a specific passage, verse, or phrase that brings you the release, the motivation, the comfort or instruction that You need. Then use that handle again and again to think the truth with thanksgiving.

In our God of perfect love, you'll find the cure you need.

—Ruth Myers in *THE PERFECT LOVE*

---

4. Follow the directions above for writing down a list of any areas in your life where you lack satisfaction and growth. Then pray over this list, as the author suggests.

We don't usually go to the expense and work of adding on to our house until we begin to feel a bit crowded. Likewise, for most of us, we don't desire greater spiritual maturity or deeper intimacy with God until we're genuinely uncomfortable and dissatisfied with where we are.

You and I both have some growing to do. Each of us has areas of immaturity in our lives, areas that we don't have to stay in. We can come out of them and move on!

Are there areas of life in which you're holding God at arm's length, so that He cannot demonstrate His personal love and desire for you? Is there any area in which your heart may be closed to His love? Have you been afraid to open it further?

Are you afraid of anything He might ask you to do? I urge you to pinpoint your fear, write it down in your own words, and present it to Him in prayer. Ask for His answer to this fear, then listen for His answer in His Word. Ask Him to work in you both to will and to do of His good pleasure — to make you willing to be willing. Keep on asking until He does it.

—Ruth Myers in *The Perfect Love*

5. Answer here the author's questions in the last two paragraphs quoted above, then follow the author's guidelines for praying over these.

6. Take time to look over each of the previous twelve lessons in this study guide.

   a. Restate here (in summary form) the most important truths about God's love that you have studied personally in this book.

   b. How would you express what you believe are the most important changes God wants to see in your life as a result of your study in this book?

7. For helpful review, write out from memory on a separate sheet of paper the passages you have memorized in this study.